# Dedication

*To my Lord and Savior the rock on which I stand, thank you for showing me that what You've deposited in me is far more valuable than the things stolen from meTo the woman that meant the world to me, Flora Jean Woods, my mother. It is because of your servitude to Jesus, the impactful legacy you left with the lives you've touched and the treasures in book form that you left me is why this book is written. To my children Jalen, Chardell, Da'shaun, Yair and Téa the reasons I understand the importance of legacy, and my prayer is that this book serves as a foundation that this family will continue to build upon. To Shawanna for believing and pushing me to run toward the vision.*

# Adam Where Are Thou?!

Understanding that this is a bit unorthodox to **put** the glossary in the front of the book. However, I am a lover of words and I believe that knowing the meaning of a word helps the writer express themselves in a manner that transitions the letter, manuscript, poem, ect. It's my personal belief that it helps the reader pinpoint the direction the author is going. By no means is this an assault on anyones intelligence, simply a way that I enjoy diving into a text.

# GLOSSARY

**Continuum-** A coherent (consistent, united) whole characterized as a collection, sequence, or progression of values or elements varying by minute degrees

**Opened- 11(A).** Having openings, interruptions, or spaces

**Passivity- C.** Lacking in energy and will. (2) Tending to not take an active or dominant part. (2)A. Not active or operating and complacency**( self satisfaction especially when accompanied by unawareness of actual dangers or deficiencies( a lack of something that is needed).**

**Placed- 6(A).** A proper or dedicated niche or setting

**C.** A distinct condition, position or state of mind

**9(B).** Prestige accorded to one of high rank

**Put-** To put into a specific place or relationship

**B.** To move in a specified direction

**D.** To bring into a specified state or condition

# Table of Contents

# Foreword

Out of the many men I've encountered with the Call of God in their life, Charlie Colston is one of the most genuine disciples and servants I have lived to witness. Adam Where Are Thou? Is a fresh look at how men have lost their authority, self-accountability, and their activity within the Kingdom of God and what they can do to change that. Colston is sounding the alarm for all men to take their place, finding their identity and destiny in God. Colston dives into Genesis, where Adam missed the mark, highlighting for us in this modern day how men surrender their authority due to a lack of ownership and accountability. Adam Where Are Thou? is a refreshing well of revelation as you will be introduced to the various things we as men can do to win back our influence and authority in the Kingdom and the modern day church.

**- Pastor Matthew D. Pyle; Teaching & Development Pastor of the Excelling Church**

# Introduction:

# Quiet whisper, Resounding echo

   Elohim (the Hebrew word for God) gave me the title of this book about five or six years ago. I had the slightest idea of where to even begin. Interestingly enough I attended a church service in which the speaker of the hour was a Prophet from Africa. This was after I had lost one of the most important and influential women in my life; my mother. He told me to search my mother's home for hidden treasures and wealth! Automatically I was thinking that maybe he was referring to her jewelry, a will or the sterling silver tea set. Neither of which I received but what I did get was her NIV Study Bible, Webster's Dictionary, Concordance and her Vine's Expository Dictionary. From the day of that prophetic word until 2019 I did not realize that the treasures and the wealth were the books! As soon as the Holy Spirit gave me that revelation I was immediately taken back to the prophecy spoken to me about this book or books as the man of God referenced. Again, as stated earlier I had not the first clue as to where or how I would start this book but let me reassure you that God will never set you on a course to accomplish a task that He himself has not completed for you. We just have to walk it out; but that's another chapter.

   I believe it was a week later after the revelation that the Father reminded me of a video that I watched of a man named Kent Hovind giving a very, very anointed explanation of God that I thoroughly enjoyed. It was so good that I thought this would be a great segue into my first topic. I will provide the video in the footnotes but first the man of God's thought provoking and anointed explanation of the existence of God.

Kent Hovind:" God is not affected by time,space or matter. In science it is called a continuum, meaning they would have to come into existence at the same time. If you have time and no space, then where would you put it? If you have space and matter but no time, then when would you put it? It has to be simultaneously. The bible answers that in 10 words:" **In the beginning (time) God created the heavens(space) and the earth (matter). Which in turn created a trinity of trinities. Time: past, present and future; Space: length, width and height; Matter: solid, liquid and gas. Thus the God that created them would have to be outside them. If He is limited by them then He is not God and if I could fit an infinite God into my 3 pound brain then He is not worth worshiping."** Let that marinate for a moment. I'm sure that you are just as amazed as I was and am.

# Chapter One

# FROM THE BEGINNING, BEGINNING

### ( THE HOLY TRINITY )

Giving the definition of continuum which we encountered, while gaining an understanding of how God exists. We also saw the words: trinity of trinities which is a great way to dive into my first topic: THE HOLY TRINITY. As far as I can remember, even from the time I first dedicated my life to Christ at 12 years old, there was never a solid explanation or understanding to the question of the GodHead. I'm going to do my best to break this down so that you may garner an understanding. Trinity : The union of the Father, Son and Holy Spirit (NOT GHOST ). From the late latin trinitat; trinatas - state of being threefold. Also the Latin word trinius- trinity. Now that we have the definition let's dig in! Elohim is the Hebrew word /name for God: God meaning the ultimate or supreme being. In Hebrew Elohim is a plural noun but it's singular in meaning when referring to God. In the book of the beginnings: Genesis 1: 26 in the first two words the emphasis of plurality was on His Deity, in verse 27 the emphasis is on the singularity of His divine substance. The very first showing of The Holy Trinity comes in the creation account. I like using accounts because it

means description of facts with synonyms such as chronicle, commentary, history, record and report. So, Elohim fashioned man out of His own image and likeness- mind, body, soul.

That's all three parts in one vessel with distinct functions. When God speaks to me He gives me a practical way to view and understand His wisdom. For instance if you are starting a new business, the Owner, CEO, Sole Proprietor is usually one person who wears many hats! Since I am Chef I'll use a restaurant or a diner for example. The Owner, Janitorial staff and Head Chef. As the owner you handle the business aspect: paperwork, payroll, set the standard and ambiance. As the Janitorial staff you're responsible for keeping the building clean and all the dishes ready for use. As the Head Chef you are responsible for checking the food order came in correctly(fresh, temperature correct and there are no damaged items). Then you have to ensure all food is cooked to industry standards and then serve the food.

You may wonder why I chose to start here; well for multiple reasons. One being to give a simplistic answer to a question a lot of believers cannot understand or explain. You can see them/Him at work from start to finish in the bible. ( creation scripture, Mary's pregnancy, Jesus' last supper and on cross.)

The second reason is to put things in their proper place, the mise en place if you will. It is us knowing who we are and whose we are. Philippians 2:13 declares: For it is[not your strength, but it is] God who is effectively at work in you, both to will and to work[ that is, strengthening, energizing, and creating in you the longing and the ability to fulfill your purpose] **for HIS good pleasure.** Lastly, it further emphasizes the call of the Father.

Genesis  1 :26-30 sets the stage to the question at hand. In these verses of scripture God created man(Adam) and gave him dominion over everything. In Genesis  2:15-20 God put/placed Adam in the Garden of Eden. Before we go any further let us examine this place and word EDEN for a moment. This place named Eden has been sought after for centuries; excavations in numerous locations around the world even thought by some to be allegory. Whatever the case, one thing remains: No one can seem to find it or anything to say it was here. After doing some research I came across another brilliant mind and anointed man of God that is sadly no longer with us but he has left a lasting impression on me. Dr. Myles Munroe gave a jewel of a  breakdown of the word;  the place named Eden. He taught that the word Eden in Hebrew has five strokes, with each stroke having a different meaning. One meaning **moment,** another **spot,** another **presence,** and the remaining two meanings are **pleasant** and **open door**.

When put together it would read something like this : **A spot for the moment where the presence of God is an open door to Heaven.** Is it a wonder that this self contained lush garden where God created everything that we are even in this day awestruck. The place man was formed from the dust of the ground, God blew His breath in man's lungs to make him a living being, HE even performed the very first surgery WITH anesthesia and created a woman(Eve) from a rib bone of Adams. Two things just jumped out at me as I typed this. 1) God did not physically touch anything until he formed Adam; HE blew HIS very essence into Adam. 2) Eve came from Adam's side( meaning to rule with him) that's another topic but **WHAT GOD DID ONCE IN ADAM HE DIDN'T HAVE TO DO TWICE IN EVE!** Meaning the authority transferred from father to son, much like when God the Father sent Jesus the Son. Also, when that transfer happened it put the onus on Adam. Is the picture becoming clearer as to why this question was asked?

**WHAT GOD DID ONCE IN ADAM HE DIDN'T HAVE TO DO TWICE IN EVE!** This point is so good that I had to repeat it twice. What does that mean? It means that God created heaven and earth, night and day, oceans, rivers and streams, fish, birds, animals and creeping things and a self-sustaining garden with trees and vegetation. Then he created man to tend to the garden, to have dominion, authority and be responsible for all that was before him. Then God gave him a command and the repercussions of not adhering to said command. God gave all this to Adam through direct lineage, He didn't have to do this with Eve because Adam was to be responsible for all that was before him and the fact Eve was made complete; she came from a complete creation. God walked with Adam in the cool of the day, Adam had direct contact, direct interaction with God. Still not clear on the question? Let's take a cognitive look at what it says in the third chapter of Genesis. It opens up describing the serpent(enemy), it goes on to describe in detail the conversation the serpent had with Eve and how she ultimately presented the forbidden fruit to Adam and he ate.

Verse seven is where the meat and potatoes are. **Then the eyes of the two of them were open.** There are two definitions of the word open that I really like: 1) **Interruptions** and 2) **Spaces**. Remember Eden: **A spot for the moment where the presence of God is a open door to Heaven.** God saw an opening, a gap, a space and said "It is not good for man to be alone." So He made Adam a help meet and blessed them. All that happened in a spot for the moment where the presence of God is a open door to heaven. After the deception of the serpent and the partaking of the fruit the command was broken and Adam created a **space** for sin and death to enter in. It caused an **Interruption** in the relationship between God and man, Creator and created, Father and son. Similarly, to when the woman with the issue of blood touched the hem of Jesus' garment through the crowd and virtue went out of Him in Luke chapter 8:43-48. Well, when Adam transgressed God felt the disconnect! He felt the interruption and came down into the garden in the cool of the day when that direct connection was most potent. Still feeling the disconnect, God asked what most good, watchful fathers would ask their beloved child when they are temporarily out of sight: Adam Where Are You? I can only imagine the tears, hurt and pain that oozed out as He walked and searched. I could imagine His face with the exact same look my mother had on her face when she saw her miracle baby wrapped up like Hannibal Lector when she came to visit me in jail. Heartbroken and devastated.

God is omniscient He knows all, omnipresent He sees all and omnipotent He is boundless. Therefore the question was more spiritual than natural. God asked where, in the sense of what have you gotten yourself into? Where are thou? I gave you a designated setting, a distinct state of mind. Where are thou? Adam I put you here; I gave you a specific position, a specified direction. Son, where are you? Because sin has touched the only thing I created and put Myself into; and because of this the connection between God and Adam can only be likened to a mother and her child. Which is why God immediately felt the interruption. Adam, where are thou?!

# Quick Jewels

What is the Gospel?

The word gospel is the Greek word Evangélio meaning good news.

Before it was written it was the oral tradition. This is why the Bible records the first four books of the New Testament as:

The Gospel according to

Matthew

Mark

Luke

John

**Synoptic Gospels**

Matthew

Mark

Luke

They are called the synoptic Gospels because they include many of the same stories, often in a similar sequence and in similar or sometimes identical wording.

Mark by John Mark, the oldest of the synoptic Gospels.

Simon Peter- had his own disciples.(John Mark).

Luke was a disciple of Paul.

The Gospel according to John is different because Matt start with lineage, Mark starts as grown Jesus, Luke starts with the birth

John starts with in the beginning

He set it up by starting with the Deity of Jesus.

**"In the beginning was the Word, and the Word was with God and the Word was God.**

**Anytime you see a word capitalized when talking about Jesus; it's Jesus.**

Logos- The word of God.

Chapter Two

# PASSIVITY

(THE SIN, THE GENERATIONAL CURSE)

You read that correctly. When reading the account of the fall which occurred in Genesis 3 there was complacency on Adam's part. Self satisfaction that was accompanied by unawareness of actual dangers. From my point of view the actual sin was Adam not being on task, not manning his post, not tending to what he was gifted. Let's make something abundantly clear; there is a stark difference between the words tend and till. Till means to prepare, cultivate, work and plow; whereas tend means to look after, direct or manage. Adam was created to tend to the garden and all it encompassed, not till it. As stated earlier the garden was self-sustaining. Adam was the watcher, yet he took his eyes off of the bride( I'm going to go into this another time.) The sin was committed before the biting of the fruit. Eating the fruit was simply the manifestation of Adam not walking in his authority and performing the duties instructed by God. The instructions were to look after the garden and Eve as well. Well, where was Adam? The bible says that Eve ate and gave to her husband who was with her. Adam failed to watch the entrance to the garden so the serpent got in. Stranger danger! He also wasn't watching Eve either, because no man or entity should be allowed to whisper in your wife's ear! The issue however, is that Adam didn't look at Eve as his wife but just another creation God had made; only this time the creation was a match for him. Adam exercised dominion over the animals of the ground, the birds of the air and the fish of the sea. Now woman which was taken from the side of man was to rule or have dominion together with man but Adam was to govern. To be the head. Yet Adam was there when Eve ate the fruit and partook of that fruit knowing what God instructed him not to do. So the eating of the fruit was the second time Adam didn't follow God's instructions to the letter. He never named Eve! He actually never gave Eve a name until after the fall and she birthed their first child. Isn't that just like us men? We never give women a name or "title" until they give us something.(I'll go deeper into this at another time.)

I know the question posed will be "How do you get this ideal of Adam being a watcher?" At the end of Genesis 3 God kicks them out of the garden and permanently places two Cherubim at the entryway (Adam's old assignment). Essentially Adam was demoted from upper level management (tend=manage), to laborer(tilling=cultivate, plowing). Passivity incubated the sin of disobedience, which bred blame shifting, embarrassment, shame, lies, jealousy, insecurities and eventually murder to name a few.

Now this brings us to the current problem at hand. The generational curse of passivity that is plaguing men in general but a vast majority of "Christian" men in their homes, ministry and in the body of Christ as a whole. We have become so passive in the area of leadership. We accept what people say and do or decide without challenging them or trying to change anything. In other words we accept what the world does, says and decides; knowing it's not right but we still will not fight it. This Adamic mindset ultimately affects the order in which God has set in place.

Let's unpack this:

Adam blame shifted, was unrepented, embarrassed and insecure after eating the fruit. Cain killed Abel because he was jealous, insecure and despised correction. Down the line Abraham had an unfounded fear of the Pharaoh because of his insecurities and lied about his wife being his sister. Further down the line Abaraham's son Issac did the exact same thing. A little further down from that Issac is deceived by his son Jacob who not only steals Esau's birthright but his blessing as well. Generational, meaning relating to the different generations of a **particular family.** You and I fall into that particular family. These sins have been handed down from father to son, mother to daughter, grandfather to grandson and so on. So what do we do?

That is the million dollar question.

It's easy to point this out but the hard part is actually dealing with the mess that not only our fathers and fathers father but the mess we created as well. My family is from Alabama, Camden to be exact. My grandparents had moved, purchased land and built a house in the amazing little town named Lower Peachtree. Man, we had a farm with cows, chickens, and acres of land for crops. There were two cow pastures. A smaller one and the main one which was HUGE. It had a pond and sometimes after feeding the cows or helping to repair the barbed wire fence I would pull some of those smooth disc like rocks out of my pocket to skip across the pond. I had a knack for finding those stones. Well, depending on where I was standing and the angle of my throw I would get 5,6,7 skips! Other times the stone would hit the water "plooop" and go to the bottom. Watch this. The objective of skipping rocks is to hit the water, bounce back up, hit the water and repeat for as long as possible. Everyone wants to skip their rocks the furthest and no one wants to hear the "plooop". It sounds dreadful. The sound lets you know that it was a failed attempt. Here's the catch; whether you skipped the rock or not you still unnaturally disturbed the water! That disturbance caused a ripple effect; it was only more pronounced when we heard the sound. Far too often we have called ourselves skipping, touching the things not of God and thinking it's okay because we bounced back up.

Part of the definition of passivity is **self satisfaction especially when accompanied by unawareness of actual dangers.** We don't realize the dangers or pay attention to the ripple effects until we hear that sound.

I know the saying is it takes two to tango but my focus is on the men. Adam was unaware of the actual dangers that presented itssself in the form of the serpent. He wasn't paying attention to the ripple effects that were forming whilst he allowed Eve to be intertwined with the serpent and then he partook as well.( I could go in on the debate on if the fruit was actual fruit but I'm going to stay the course). It wasn't until he heard the **sound** of God's footsteps as He walked in the garden during the cool of the day. It wasn't until he heard the **sound** of God calling out to him that he knew he messed up. So here we are some 5,000 years later still dealing with touching the things God told us not to touch, not being in position or playing our position, still being passive, and still hearing the sound of God's footsteps as he approaches and hearing the voice of a sad and heartbroken  father calling out asking us "Where are we?" Where is our mindset? Where is our authority? Where is our desire to be in the Father's will? 1 John 2:15 says: Love not the world, neither the things that are in the world. If any man loves the world, the love of the Father is not in him. Yet we will follow celebrities on social media, go to secular artist shows, go hard to make music with secular artists, we do their dances, participate in the worldy pagan rituals and be quick to say someone save because they say god, heaven, halleluYah, or

amen. Make it make sense. The sad part is that we can find a thousand excuses as to why it's ok but not once did we or do we ask the Most High if He's ok with it. The simple truth is that we know He isn't. We're so passive that we don't even try the spirit by the spirit.

Don't you find it strange that you very seldom hear adjectives like devout when describing "christians"? We have become so passive that it's scary. Name another belief system that allows all that we allow into our homes, lives and even our places of worship. I cannot even tell you how over it I am with churches remixing worldly songs and pretending it's ok because they added the words God and Jesus; as if the Messiah is seated on the right hand of the Father bobbing His head in approval. Passive! Gospel singers doing songs with secular artists connecting them to your audience but never winning souls on their side. Passive! I can go on about grown men wearing skirts and singing "gospel" and snoop dogg making "gospel" music but still calling women female dogs and crip walking but that's the Passive church; headed by passive men. I digress. I will say this, take a serious moment to ask the Most High "How is my walk with you"? The bible says God's word is sharper than any two-edged sword; meaning His word is cutting me too! You're not alone in the chastisement I pray you are feeling. I am really going in on this aspect because I was an inspiring hip hop artist.

I even did some christian hip hop with my best friend; we did a song called "Confident Christian" over a Rick Ross instrumental. I for one thought and think that the song is dope. However, when I really think about it, those lyrics on that instrumental was like putting ice cream on top of rat poisoning. No matter how good the lyrics were, when the instrumental was made the **intent** behind it wasn't to give God glory. I had to repent for that because that is nothing more than me being double minded, having one foot in church and the other in the world.

## *Quick Jewels*

*Did you know that the Great God we serve laid out His redemptive plain through these people in ten generations?!*

*It's all in the meanings of their names!*

*Adam begat Seth*

*Seth begat Enosh*

*Enoch begat Kenan/Cainan*

*Kenan/Cainan begat Mahalalel*

*Mahalalel begat Jared*

*Jared begat Enoch*

*Enoch begat Methuselah*

*Methuselah begat Lamech*

*And*

*Lamech begat Noah*

*Adam=Man*

*Seth=Appointed*

*Kenan/Cainnan=Sorrow*

*Mahalalel=The Blessed God*

*Jared=Shall come down*

*Enoch=Teaching*

*Methuselah=His death shall bring*

*Lamech=The despairing*

*Noah=Rest(Comfort)*

*[I noticed that **selah** was at the end of Methuselah's name. I found it interesting and decided to look it up. Some of the meanings are: stop, think on this/ to pause/ let this sink in/ dually noted and my favorite- **Forever.**]*

*So when putting it all together  it reads something like this:* **Man** *has been* **Appointed Mortal Sorrow; but The Blessed God, Shall Come Down Teaching,  and His Death Shall Forever Bring The Despairing Rest(Comfort).**

*This blew my mind! I pray this has blessed you as much as it has blessed me. Amen.*

Chapter Three

# LONGING TO RECONNECT

## (A Father's Love)

In 2010 I came home from prison on March 31st . I came back with a vengeance; smoking, drinking, partying and fornicating trying to make up for 5 years of lost time. Within a few months things got bad. I had gotten stabbed and could have died and my oldest two children moved to Tampa Florida with their mom; but then something amazing happened. I began to go with my best friend to a gathering called "Love Jar" hosted by a young believer named Lysa whom we met earlier during the summer. The way the function was set up was we would gather around the table like a family, have a delicious dinner and allow God to have His way. Sometimes it would be the simple medicine of laughter at jokes and pranks or board and card games. Other times it would be reading scriptures, testimonies given and all out praise and worship. I'm talking about adoration of The Most High God, crying, snot blowing, laying prostrate worship and prophetic words spoken over the people. It was a small basement in Hollis, Queens that drew leaders in the kingdom and believers in all stages of their walk in the faith together in one accord.

That was wednesday night and then we began to go to midnight prayer in Brooklyn on friday hosted by the now Bishop Courtney Bradley.

Some of you are reading and may be wondering why I am telling you this and how it fits into the overall story of Adam, Eve, the serpent, the garden and God? The aim is to point out how and when God began to pour Himself into my life little by little and how He began to reestablish a connection with a grandchild of Adam. Being poured into, from these two life changing gatherings that I truly got excited over and looked forward to attending in late 2010. I did this to point out that knowing your timeline is of utmost importance, so much so that God gave us His throughout the bible. God's stance or position has remained consistent from Genesis to Revelations. Longing to have a personal connection, relationship with us. Sadly, our position has switched back and forth from obedience and love to disobedience, rebellion and sin. Looking at this word position, **everything that a man loves he requires for it to be in a position.** I'll prove it to you. **We love sports, sports require the athletes to play or be in a certain position, "friends" we keep them in a certain position in our life, jobs we apply for because of a position, sex———————; yeah, you get the picture. So we as men require for all things in our life to be in or play a certain position. My question is: "Why doesn't it apply to us?"**

We vie for position in our homes, on jobs, in sports and even in ministry yet when it comes to God we frequently make excuses as to why we are not in position. "The bible has been tampered with", "the church is too soft and caters to women" and blah, blah, blah. We have more excuses than a person going to jail. The truth is we have most often missed the first position in God. That position is to have knees bent and back bowed in His presence. In Luke chapter 18 and verse 1 Jesus gives the disciples a parable to show them that men should always pray and faint not. What is the posture of prayer? Knees bent and head bowed because it shows a position of submitting to a Power greater than ourselves! Arguing over the word submit or submittance is word schematics at best and at worst it's a person who is not fully committed to Christ. The book of John 15:4-11 tells us what it's like and the benefits of being submitted to God. *"Abide in me, and I in you. As the branch cannot bear fruit of itself, unless it abides in the vine, neither can you, unless you abide in me."*

**Abide- to accept or act in accordance with( a rule, decision or recommendation). Submit- accept or yield to a SUPERIOR force or to the AUTHORITY or WILL of another person.** We have an issue when we take a worldly understanding or connotation of a word or words to explain or build an argument against why we can't submit to God. Sadly, we will submit to the wills of our bosses on our secular jobs,

and submit to the wills of the bill collectors when they say it's time to pay up. Yet when it comes to being submitted to the Creator we continue to choose the created. Let's dig a little deeper into the action of submitting. What does it mean to submit? One of the meanings is to play it by the book. The book= the **BIBLE** gives us instructions on how to carry ourselves, live, eat, conduct business, treat each other, community service, marriage, parenting, being a good friend, being a believer and so on and so forth. A common statement that is often said is" if you broke one commandment then you've broken them all."

If you cannot submit; play it by the book then you cannot keep in step in the other areas of life. The opposite of submit is to defy! Everyone has had or even have a vice. We will yield to it but not to God. Whether we like it or not our closeness and elevation in Christ depends on our willingness to submit to God. Again we can argue, debate and agree to disagree over using the word submit when speaking of God because "men don't like to use that word", "I'm a man, submit sounds soft." Yet those same men are not willing to be whipped, speared and crucified like Christ, or stoned like Stephen, Paul was stoned to near death, got up and continued his journey to preach the gospel. Is that soft? Many men reading this will say why is he going so hard? It's simple; I'm trying to break a mindset that has had (US) bound and straddling the fence for far too long! Come Out!

James chapter 4: 7-8, 10 gives instructions to submit. Being humbled like 2 Chronicles 7:14-16 not only states what God requires but gives the benefits of that submittance. This is a Selah moment.

We require so much of God and He requires very little in return. Even when it comes to faith He only asks for that to be mustard seed size. You inheriting the Kingdom of God and receiving full benefits without submitence is equal to receiving prophecy with no instructions. It's not going to happen. Every day that God allows us to open our eyes is His grace giving us another opportunity to reconnect with Him. I know you've sinned and made a mess of things, so have I. I know you don't feel worthy. Here's a transparent moment: It took years for me to utter "HalleluYah" to the Father; I felt so ashamed, so dirty and disgusting, not worthy of giving God the highest praise. Imagine being in church and even serving in ministry and being so broken in your mind and heart because the enemy is projecting his life sentence over you? So much so that the highest praise that you can give The Most High God won't even move past your lips. That was me, but Romans 5:20 declares- Moreover the law entered that the offense might abound. But where sin abounded, grace abounded much more. Trust I know what it feels like to feel that you've been abandoned, to have lost hope, to feel like life isn't worth living, to feel like nothing you do matters, that you don't make a difference.

I know what it feels like to feel hollow inside. That missing piece is **RELATIONSHIP** with Christ. Long to reconnect with Him as He longs to reconnect with us. Get to know Him more. In my opinion God is not looking for you and I to be sinless but for us to sin-less than we did the day before. 2 Corinthians 9:8 says "And God is able to make all grace abound toward you, that you, always having all sufficiency in all things, may have an abundance for every good work." No one wants to be inadequate and the only way to not be is by doing the work.

# Quick Jewels

## NAMES OF GOD

*Calling **God** by His name requires an answer.*

***Yahweh**- The Lord, God (the covenant name of God, the holiest of names. It is derived from the hebrew "I am")*

***Adonai**- Lord God, Master(the name is the plural form of adon=Lord. The plurality of it is a direct reference to the Trinity.)*

***Elohim**- Father God, God the Creator(I love this name because it is a glorification of His absolute power and sovereignty.)*

***Yehovah Yireh**- The Lord will provide( I feel the need to dig into this name a little more. Firstly I know many are looking at my spelling of God's name in this fashion; well, during the time period of the written word the letter "J" didn't exist. That wasn't until 1524 when an Italian man named Gian Giorgio Trissino invented it. Now onto the good part. The name is only mentioned once and that is in Genesis 22, the account of father Abraham being instructed to sacrifice his son Isaac. God stopped him and provided a ram instead. )*

***Yehovah Rapha*** *- The God who heals(this name not only reveals God's power to heal, repair and rejuvenate those physical areas of our lives but penetrate to the core of your spirit as well.)*

***El Roi*** *- The God who sees me(Given to God by Hagar when He spoke to her in the midst of her despair and wailing grief.)*

***El Elyon*** *- The name Elyon is a combination of two words. El is a name of God that means strength, might, or power; and Elyon in Hebrew means to ascend or go up. When combined the two names literally translate to the Extremely-Exalted, Sovereign, High God.*

***El Echad*** *- The One God(Echad meaning one in Hebrew)*

***El Tsaddik*** *- The Righteous God(Tsaddik meaning righteous)*

***El Olam*** *- God Everlasting, The Everlasting God(Olam meaning world, universe, everlasting time or space.)*

***El Gibbor*** *- The Mighty God(Gibbor means strong and mighty; a picture of God as a Warrior and Champion.)*

**These are just a few Names of God. Some known and some not but the purpose is to give an understanding of the Names and how they honor God and reflect our cry, need, and dependency on God for EVERYTHING.**

## Chapter Four

# UNACCOUNTABILITY

### (Our Achilles Heel)

Here is a reason we tend to fall and become accustomed to being lukewarm. Now I know this is a everybody thing but I am specifically addressing the men, the elect of the Adamic covenant. The first covenant. In Genesis 3:12 Adam opened the door for the judgment that we are still living with today. Not only did he sin against God but he didn't even repent. He didn't hold himself accountable. He said " The woman whom thou gavest me……" , even though God gave the instructions to him first before Eve was even created. Unaccountability places us in a space where our growth is stunted. Our growth in life, meaningful relationships and most of all with the Father. No amount of success can replace being able to look in the mirror and allow God to make the necessary changes in our lives. It's easy to point out what's wrong in the lives of others but the hardest thing to do is evaluate ourselves. I have a saying "Self reflection affects the reflection in the mirror." It means that when you can go through the process of analyzing yourself, seeing what needs to be changed and actually work on them. It starts with you.

A question that I've been asked a lot as of late is "What does that look like?" The bible says that King David was a man after God's own heart. Why? The reason is that David wasn't afraid to hold himself accountable. Regardless of how messed up the situation was, how hard the fall was, he was never too proud or too high strung to go to God and humbly repent. When you look at it, that was one of the major distinctions between him and his predecessor Saul.

Do you know that unaccountability will make you miss out on some of the greatest moments, opportunities, assignments and people whose life you were predestined to reach in your lifetime? Look at the exchange Abraham had with God before Sodom and Gahmorra were destroyed. Elohim allowed Abraham to go down to only 10 people who were righteous or morally accountable in order to put away His wrath. The cities were destroyed. Another thing that happens when you fail to be held accountable it breeds a spirit of offense; where anything that's said is automatically offensive. As a kid when my mother sent me to live on that farm in Alabama with my grandparents there was two things you could be sure of 1) my grandmother was going to have TBN(Trinity Broadcasting Network) on tv at all times and 2) the local gospel radio station was going to play in the cars at all times. I remember hearing a song one day by a group called the Canton Spirituals and they had a song with the lyrics "Sweep around your own front door, before you try to sweep around mine".

See operating in the Spirit of Offense won't allow you to listen to a song like that and definitely not read Luke 6:42 " Or how can you say to your brother, 'Brother, let me remove the speck that is in your eye,' when you yourself do not see the plank that is in your own eye? Hypocrite! First remove the plank from your own eye, and then you will see clearly to remove the speck that is in your brother's eye. This behavior is why we have the blind leading the blind. If you have a plank that is blocking your vision and you still attempt to remove my speck, puncturing or rupturing my vision now we both cannot see.

Being unaccountable will have you weighing sins or wrongs. "Well, what you did was far more hurtful than what I did to you" or "That didn't bother/hurt you". Yet we are quick to say the most famous line in the unaccountable arsonal "I'm Not Perfect" but you require everyone else to be when it comes to you. Listen, you cannot be right or get right with God if you don't submit and be willing to be held accountable. Repentance is holding yourself accountable. The word says in Philippians, work out your own salvation in fear and trembling. Be accountable. Lastly, I sub titled this chapter Our Achilles Heel because along with the other two things mentioned in this chapter pride is the culmination of them all.

Pride comes before the fall. Many men have fallen to pride. We are in the spiritual war we're in because one angel got filled with pride, deceived one woman who introduced the deception to one man who broke the first command God gave in the garden to man.

Let's rewind and get a clearer picture. God formed man out of the dust of the ground, breathed into his nostrils the breath of life; and man became a living soul. No command. God then planted a garden eastward of Eden. No command. And there He put the man whom He had formed. No command. And out of the ground made the Lord God to grow every tree that is pleasant to the sight, and good for food; the tree of life also in the midst of the garden, and the tree of the knowledge of good and evil. No command. Then God created and named the four rivers and then He took man in the garden to dress it and to keep it. Then BOOM! Command: And the Lord God commanded the man, saying, Of every tree of the garden thou mayest freely eat: but the tree of the knowledge of good and evil, thou shalt not eat of it: for in the day that thou eatest thereof thou shalt surely die. Genesis 2:4-17. Are you wondering why I wrote it this way? I did it to show that very important component of accountability- Listening. God gave us two ears and one mouth; to listen more than we speak. If you refuse to do that you'll refuse to hold yourself to the exact same standards you require of everyone else. Even though God is God all by Himself a decision to partner with man was made. Many of us desire the closeness and security of a partnership but refuse to hold ourselves to the same standards. Unaccountability, unrepentance and the inability to take constructive criticism leads to doors being unhinged. In this context the doors are your boundaries. Zero boundaries equals All-Access. The serpent gained access he shouldn't have had. God removed Adam and Eve for all the things stated earlier and because He could not build the desired partnership with those deficiencies.

# <u>Quick Jewels</u>

## The Pentateuch

Which is a Greek word meaning five books or volume of five, refers to what is known collectively by the Jews as the Torah. The collective of books that make up the Torah are:

**Genesis**

**Exodus**

**Leviticus**

**Numbers**

**Deuteronomy**

Like the Holy God that inspired these writings, the Bible is full of nuggets. The word **TORH** is spelled out in every 49th letter in Genesis and Exodus. The format skips Leviticus and picks back up Numbers and Deuteronomy but spelled **HROT**. If you're anything like me then you're wondering why. Well, further digging reveals that **ALL LANGUAGES FLOW TOWARD JERUSALEM.** East of Jerusalem write right to left. West of Jerusalem write left to right. However, when examining Leviticus studies show that every 7th letter spells **YHWH**. Showing that the **TORH** always points back to **Adonai**.

I pray this has blessed you as much as it has me. Amen.

Chapter Five

# DO YOU KNOW?

### (Who You Are?)

In the last chapter we touched on God creating man on the 6th day. This happens in Genesis 2:7. And the Lord God _formed_ man out of the _dust_ of the ground; let's pause right here. The Hebrew word for formed is yâtsâr or yaw-tsâr meaning to mould into a form especially as a potter; according to The New Strong's Complete Dictionary of Bible Words #3335. In this same book the word for dust is âphâr meaning earth, mud and clay. Stay with me. I'm going somewhere. So God created man on the 6th day, molding or fashioning him out of the earth, mud and clay. Another word for earth or dirt is soil. Upon further research I've found there are six types of soil and they all have their pros and cons.

Here they are:

6. Clay- easy to distinguish, lumpy and sticky when it's wet. The biggest problem is that it is horrible at draining and has no air pockets but provides plenty of nutrients.

5. Sandy- feels gritty in your hands, it warms up fast and drains well but it's not as fertile as other soils and the nutrients drain away quickly.

4. Silty- feels soft in your hands like soap. It holds moisture well and rich in nutrients but it can become compacted or compressed. Root plants cannot grow here and this soil can get waterlogged easily.

3. Peaty- has a dark color when wet, it feels damp and spongy. It heats up quickly, rich in nutrients, slows down decomposition but it's highly acidic and retains a lot of water.

2. Chalky- has larger grains and a stony feel. It's a champion at draining but it's alkaline so some acid is needed to balance it and it leaches out iron and magnesium.

I did the breakdown this way to save the best for last!

1. Loamy- It is a mixture of Clay, Silt and Sand. The texture is fine and a bit damp. It is the ideal soil and has a great structure for planting. Nutrients are held well and drain off at a moderate rate.

Wait a minute, so you mean to tell me that on the 6th day God looked at six different soil types that were all good for growth but chose the three that mostly resemble Him, the Son and the Holy Spirit. Mixed them together, molded it, breathed the breath of life into it and made the perfect living and breathing garden?! Where Jesus plants, the Holy Spirit waters and the Father gets the increase!

Who are you? Do you know? I believe that you and I were created, formed, fashioned out of loamy soil. Able to be molded, retain and drain off water, and is perfectly structured for planting and growing. Our bodies are made up of 70% water; yet we have multiple ways to drain off water. The bible says "so as a man thinketh, so is he". Meaning whatever we plant in our minds will grow. Good and Bad alike. We were made in His image and likeness and given dominion over the things of the earth. We are God's representatives on this earth, the physical embodiment of His Kingdom. Why do you think that the enemy is fighting you so hard in your mind, in your home, in your relationship, your marriage, your finances and your church home? It's because he knows that once this mind in you is like the mind of Christ Jesus (Yahshua) then you will walk in the power and dominion given to you. Even by reading this you're making headway in taking your power back! My desire with this book has been to plant into your spirit who God has created you to be. The Bible says that God's word is sharper than any two-edged sword, meaning it cuts both ways. This book is convicting and helping me as much as it's helping you. I am not exempt!

There are major steps that have to be taken in order for us to get back to dominion and power. This next statement I am taking from a book written by the Founder and Executive Chairman of the World Economic Forum.

Klaus Schwab's book ( The Great Narrative: For a Better Future) says this on page 20: " Narrative shapes our perception and forms our reality. It influences our choices and actions, helping us find meaning in life." I know on the surface this quote is focused on a financial aspect but again that's on the surface. However, when we look at it closely what sticks out is **"Narrative shapes our perception and forms our reality "**. Isn't that what happened in Eden? The serpent redirected the narrative which not only changed Adam and Eve's perception of God's command but ultimately their reality. "I hid because I was naked." A distortion of the truth is a **lie[ a boldface one; get it?]**.

My questions to you are: What lie has the enemy told you that has changed the narrative of your life , altered your perception and more importantly are you ready to take it ALL back? The first thing we have to do is **submit and repent**. I consider this being one in the same because when you submit to God, repentance follows because you want to be in the Most High's will. We spoke on and gave the definition to the word submit. Long gone are the days of simply being connected to the extension cord; we are focused on connecting ourselves to the source Yahovah. This is the moment, this is the time, reposition yourself in Christ.

# Quick Jewels

(Why God Rested)

God rested on the Sabbath not because He was tired or that He needed to take a break. I was literally because He finished His work. Genesis 2:2-3 says: And on the seventh day Yahweh ended His work which He had made: and He rested on the seventh day from **ALL** His work which He had made. And Yahweh **blessed** and **sanctified** it. What does that mean you ask? It means that Elohim's work included: The fall, The murder of Able, The Exodus, The plagues, His commandments, laws and precepts, The flood, Israel's bondage, His endless love which manufactured grace, mercy, and His redemptive plan through the sacrifice of His only begotten Son, the fulfillment of all prophecies, the tribulation to come and The Messiah's reign at the end of days. They were all completed when He rested.

In Jeremiah 29:11 it says: For I know the thoughts I have toward you, saith the Lord, thoughts of peace, and not of evil, to give you an **expected** end. That is an added benefit to our lives knowing that God wrote our beginning from the end. How amazing is that? The Father is standing in our future, showing us how He brought us through our past and is actively working in our present time!

In Philippians 1:6 the Apostle Paul said: Being confident in this very thing, that He who has begun a good work in you is faithful to perform it until the day of Jesus Christ. It is already done for you and I.

# Chapter Six

# WORK WHILE IT'S DAY

## (It Is Now or Never)

The book of John 9:4-5 says: **I must work the works of Him who sent me, while it is day: the night cometh, when no man can work. As long as I am in the world, I am the light of the world.** This was Jesus' (Yahshua's) response to the disciples as they passed the man that was blind from birth and they asked Him who sinned the man or his parents? Further reading we know that Jesus (Yahshua) spat on the ground, made clay and **anointed** the eyes of the blind man. The structure of my writing is very intentional; hence the parenthesis and bold lettering. I do this to put emphasis on what I'm saying. The Messiah's response to the disciples wasn't simply about Him. That is for us too! To my understanding it was more of instructions and empowerment coming from the second Adam. In that moment 100% GOD and 100% man was shown. He acknowledges that God created Him for a purpose, that He only had a limited time to do it and that He was the light of the world as long as He was here. 100% man. Isaiah 28:10 says For precept *must be* upon precept, precept upon precept, Line upon line, line upon line, Here a little, there a little.

The 100% GOD comes in because that statement was also a command. How? In Matthew chapter 5:14-16 reads as follows: 14) Ye are the light of the world. A city that is set on a hill cannot be hid. 15) Neither do men light a candle, and hid it under a bushel, but on a candlestick; and it giveth light unto all that are in the house. 16) Let your light shine before men, that they may see your good works, and **glorify your Father which is in heaven.** Ecclesiastes 3 tells us there is an appointed time for everything. Jesus also tells us in John 14:12 that those of us who believe will do the **works** He did and greater. Works meaning healing of the sick, raising the dead, feeding the poor, taking care of the widows, teaching and preaching the gospel. Not walking on water because that wasn't works; and greater meaning we have a longer time period to do the works. Jesus had three years and charged a people and changed the world. God promises us 70 years, 80 in strength; so, what's your excuse?

When we go a little further into the scripture of John 9 we read that Jesus forms clay out of the dirt He spit on but here's where things change. The Bible says that Jesus anointed the man's eyes. As previously stated in the earliest part of the book I love words so it was super interesting that the Bible used the Hebrew word masah which transliterates to anoint. Theoretically the meaning of the word masah is fourfold. The first meaning that a person or object is set apart for divine use like King Solomon in 1 Chronicles 29:22.

Second, when people were anointed, God empowered them to accomplish His task like the Prophet Samuel in 1 Samuel 10:6. Thirdly, no one was/is allowed to harm God's anointed that's in 1 Samuel 24:10 and 26:9. Lastly, the word mashiyach #4899 derives from masah and refers to Israel's Messiah who was to come from the house of David. Make it make sense, you say? Sure, the man was blind since birth and Jesus told the disciples it wasn't sin that caused it. Jesus Himself being the Messiah, set apart for divine use and empowered by God to accomplish or complete successfully His task used one of the very elements ( clay) that I mentioned in the last chapter to give this man sight. The man didn't go blind, he came into the world blind and Jesus the 100% God gave him sight literally! Formed his sight out of the very dirt used to create the man himself! Not to bring up old stuff and I love Pastor Mike Todd but the reason that visual didn't go over well is because he was not set apart to do that. Only God is qualified to make man or any of his faculties out of dirt. Likewise, you didn't read of the disciples walking on water after Jesus ascended (insert Shrug emoji). The point being we are missing the instructions and move of God because one: not being in position and two: we're not doing the work.

Here's my belief on why we aren't doing the work . When you read the bible from Genesis all the way through Revelations one of the things that is abundantly clear is that God, the people He hand picked, the Prophets, Jesus and the Apostles dealt with the past, moved in the present but kept their eyes on the future, Whew! That's a word. Genesis starts chapter one " In the beginning", that denotes history- the account of our past. When we get to chapter 6 the bible talks about all the wickedness in the world. God picks Noah in that present time to save his family and the animals so when the Father's wrath hits the earth the future could be secured. This is shown throughout the bible. Likewise, we need to remember what and where the Most High brought us from(our past), deal with/ work on whatever is happening in our now(present: which is truly that- a gift) but consult and hear God so we may walk into our next(future).

# *Quick Jewels*

*The pour comes in when you are walking with your leader when everyone has deserted them.*

*There should be a level of mentorship there in the way it was with Elijah and Elisha, a level of brotherhood that resembles the Apostle Paul and Silas , moreover, a bond so close that your spirit does like the Bible describes David and Jonothan's bond as being knitted together. That is also the way we should be with our Lord and Savior. Proverbs 18:24 says:" A man that has friends must himself be friendly, But there is a friend who sticks closer than a brother." That friend is Jesus. You can tell Him all about your issues, struggles and everything in between. The word says He knows the number of hairs on our head! Now that's paying attention to detail. Brothers there is nothing that we can go through that God doesn't already know, but guess what? He already had the plan in place! 1 Corinthians 10:13 says "No temptation has overtaken you except what is common to mankind, And God is **faithful**; He will not let you be tempted beyond what you can bear. But when you are tempered, He will also **provide a way out so you can endure**." So not only are you not alone in those situations but you have God and He has blessed you with a brotherhood AND a way of escape! You don't have to go through this alone.*

## Chapter Seven

# VITAL IMPORTANCE

## (It's Bigger Than You/ A Call To Alignment)

As I was thinking of a way to open up this chapter I opened my Bible and began reading the New International Version(NIV) of Genesis and before the chapter starts it gives an intro breaking down how Genesis is a part of the Torah, the first five books of the bible or what is called the books of Moses. Which is a great opening; however, the ending of the intro caught my attention. It reads: the story of human history and the beginning of *God's plan to restore humanity and their place in His world.* That is the sum total of why this book was written. To point out that this is God's desire for your life and I've been given the task of helping the man reading this  begin the work of repositioning, walking in authority and breaking generational curses.

Let's reposition by first getting into a posture of prayer and giving **EVERYTHING** over to the one that is making intercession in heaven on our behalf, Jesus(Yahshua). In John 14 verse 6 He says that He is the way, the truth and the life. No one comes to the Father except through me. So we lay everything down at His feet; broken marriages, broken finances, broken hearts, broken friendships, broken family bonds, past deeds we've done that God has already forgiven us for but the enemy won't let us let it go. We have to lay down the lies, lay down that lustful spirit, that spirit of pride; those thoughts of not being enough. Lay down the thoughts of being alone and no one understands. Let's give it to him. I encourage you to lay it down in prayer; He'll meet you right where you are. Every past trauma that makes you secretly question your manhood, question your authority, question if the Father hears you. That makes you question if there is power in you or even in the name of Jesus. My brother I have labored through this book to ensure you that there is power in the name of Jesus!

Listen, I first gave my life to Christ at 12 years old, it was exhilarating, I felt so alive and free. It didn't last long because not one person taught me that it was the relationship with the Messiah that I needed to ensure that I stayed that way. I hadn't realized how much that affected me until now as I'm writing this. After I rededicated my life to Christ after I came home from prison I could say a lot in worship. "Thank you Jesus," "I love you Father", "You're mighty and worthy to be praised". Yet I couldn't give Him the highest praise. I couldn't say "HalleluYah" because I felt I was not good enough to say it, too dirty to say it. After ALL He brought me through, the enemy had me bound so I would just call on Jesus; and pray and cry and wonder what was wrong with me. Guess what?

After dealing with that turmoil, dealing with losing my parents; my father before I got married and my mother 8 months later three days after my birthday. Losing a host of aunts, uncles, cousins, one of my older brothers(making it about 20 relatives) and my marriage right after that, all in a six year period. I backslide yet again.  Now those things were piled on top of: Being born premature and not breathing at all and because of that after receiving God's breath of life my frail body was wracked with grand mal seizures. They were so bad and out of control that my family would place spoons in my mouth to keep me from biting my tongue off; so bad that my fevers would be so high they had to give me ice baths just to regulate my temperature, asthma and sleep apnea but my mother and grandparents kept calling on the name of Jesus! Even in my backslidden state I would call on the name of Jesus. I've made out of situations that I Know God did it. Selling drugs one night a rival drug dealer sent an addict to purchase from me and lure me out of the driveway I was in, into the street to blow my head off. I stopped abruptly at the edge of the driveway before the sidewalk met the street.

BOOM! It sounded like a canon. I know now that God sent His angels to stop me in my tracks; had they not you wouldn't be reading this. I've survived being t-boned on my driver's side by a car doing 60 mph. It pushed the truck a quarter of a block; I got out the driver's side door. The police arrived, tried to open the door and couldn't; they called me a liar.

The entire bar was outside and told them I was telling the truth. They witnessed a miracle. I got stabbed in my side, rushed to the hospital, laid up in the hospital for three days. The doctor called me lucky, said if the knife was 2 ½ inches longer it would have punctured my small intestines and there wouldn't have been anything they could have done; given the way and time I arrived at the ER. I'm here today because I was so depressed and broken, financially, spiritually and emotionally. Child support was draining me and I felt hopeless. My job at the time would give you a $10,000 life insurance plan once hired. All that week I smoked weed and read my bible that my mom gave me. My last day of work for the week was thursday. I did my regular routine except this time after I smoked I was trying to figure out a way to commit suicide and still get the policy paid out to my children. In my mind something beats nothing and they'd be better off without me.

I fell asleep and God woke me up saying "REPENT FOR THE KINGDOM OF HEAVEN IS AT HAND". I woke up sweating, heart pounding and did exactly that. I came to Long Island after being on my face(literally) before the Lord for two weeks; just to see my babies start "Big Kids" school which was pre-k and k. I couldn't leave. Every time I tried something came up. The children asked me to come to church with them and I did.

I met my now Pastor, Prophet Garelle K. Solomon and he prophesied about that night that I wanted to end it all. At that time no one knew. I spoke that to not a soul. He told me that the reason God wouldn't let me do it was because He had GRACE stamped on my chest. I'm giving you this testimony to tell you that God has not left you, that His word concerning you will not return unto Him void, but it will accomplish all He set it out to do. I am living proof. He is El Roi the God that sees you and He is longing to reestablish you, restore you and reaffirm you as the Priest of your home, as a husband, a father, a friend, a son, a brother, a minister, a pastor. Whatever He has called you to do and become. However, that restoration process starts with doing the work of reposturing and repositioning ourselves.

After that we relearn how to put on the whole armor of God, that ye may be able to stand against the wiles of the devil. Now it's time to get our power back. A part of that is knowing that without God we're nothing, yet He's still God without us. This life we have been given is for His good pleasure as was written earlier in the book. It is not our own. Knowing that will make room for the savior to use us as His vessel; a conduit into which He can show Himself mighty connecting His SUPER to our natural; I like to call it being plugged into the source of the power and not the extension cord. But that only comes through a relationship with Him. Getting into His word, learning His precepts. Let's be honest, most of us are not giving a stranger a new car, house, business or $100,000 to someone we don't know. So why expect that from the Father? When we are talking about putting on the armor we should look at David. Before David finally convinced Saul that he was indeed capable of defeating Goliath, Saul tried to put his armor on David. It was too heavy for him to wear99 let alone go into a battle of **life or death**. Herein lies the problem we have as men; far too often we try to wear who or what someone says that we are. Regardless of the boxing in, four things will emerge when your mind is focused on the kingdom. 1) You'll realize that the only person that knows you better than you is God. 2) Man can only **truly call you or title you what God has already spoken in the Heavenlies.** 3) You'll understand your purpose once you accept your assignment. 4) Coveting someone else's assignment(wife, family, career, position, etc.) will cause more heartache and pain than joy. I once received a revelation that was simply stated: "physical obedience brings spiritual release." Meaning how we live, maneuver, and follow instructions from the Father determines the release date of blessings, answered prayers and even the move and presence of God in our particular or specific situation(s). Looking back at number three above, I mentioned purpose. Now it is automatic that men in general and especially believers talk about and strive to achieve their purpose. I'm not God so I cannot give an exact number of times the question of "What's my purpose?" has been asked to and of Him. I do know that in the different circles I've been in it has been a question oft asked and seldom answered. I've come to the conclusion that a vital component has gone missing or perhaps overlooked. That component is the Priesthood. Yes! Far too often we put our purpose over our Priesthood. We are a generation and nation that has this Malcolm X mentality when it comes to fulfilling purpose: **By Any Means Necessary!** Not only did it eventually cost him his life, it also put the very people he said he loved in mortal danger but it didn't start with him and it didn't start with you or your father or your father's father. It started in the garden too! Adam was so absorbed by his purpose that he didn't even realize God gave him Priesthood first. With Yahweh being the **Ultimate Priest** He did so in four steps. 1) He created Adam in His image and likeness. 2) He blew His essence, the breath of life into the created being to give him life. 3) He gave him a (help meet) wife. 4) He blessed them. Then He gave Adam purpose! Be fruitful and Subdue the earth. If the focus was on the Priesthood that was transferred from the Almighty in the form of the **Ruach** as well as being given a help meet then he would have automatically fulfilled purpose by subduing and having dominion over the serpent whom he allowed to whisper to his wife.

Let me make this abundantly clear. If you're married, engaged, dating with a purpose or even divorced: **HOME IS YOUR FIRST MINISTRY.** I don't care what anyone says. That fact that this has been overlooked so egregiously is shameful. Many divorces, separations and breakups have happened because of unhealthy balances between your first ministry and the ministry of the church. If I could take an educated guess(hypothesis) I would say that it isn't just a now thing but it has been an issue. Why? Well look at how the church was discussed BC(Before Christ) the focus was on the physical temple. Then Jesus comes along and says that the temple is internal! "Destroy this temple and I'll raise it up in three days". In short, you cannot keep God's house in order if yours is in disarray.

That wouldn't be decent and in order. Even an airplane stewardess will tell you in case of a crash landing, you put on your oxygen mask first before you help someone else. We have to stop moving backwards.  My brethren, this is my part two to the clarion call given in chapter six. Our Savior, our Redeemer, our Intercessor who makes petitions on our behalf and our Brother with whom we are joint heirs to the throne is coming back expecting for us to be in our proper places. For us to be positioned in Him. As I'm writing this, the lyrics to the Winans song tomorrow is running through my mind. I don't want any problems so I won't write the lyrics but if you haven't heard it listen to it.

Jesus our soon coming King is expecting us, man, His Father's crowning jewel to not just be in position but to be in right standing because **hell** is a real place but it was not built for us. We have a choice to hear **"Depart from me I know you not" or "Well done my good and faithful servant."** He's given us free will to choose. I won't lie and say that if you choose the latter that it won't come with hurts, heartaches and pain but there is a scripture God gave me in a dream while I was in the box/shu (special housing unit. Away from population when you get in trouble) in prison. It was a HUGE book with the brightest white pages and it had bullet points and writing. I knew without the shadow of a doubt it was the bible. It had no book name and no verse numbers but the bullet points and the writing was the richest black ever created. I was in the box with no contact with anyone when I received the scripture through a letter from my mom that arrived the following day. It was Psalms 30: 5b-" Weeping may endure for a night, but joy cometh in the morning." This transition is tough but necessary not just for us but for our children and children's children.

I didn't desire or need this to be a long read, my greatest desire has been from the start is for this writing to be majorly impactful. To bring about a shifting in our posture, to regain the authority given in the form of a blessing by our Creator.

Digest that for a minute. It was and is a BLESSING from GOD to be the priest, the head, upper management of all created, the lender and leader. He gave us the green light to operate in *that blessing.* We haven't fully grasped that but we're asking for more blessings; but I digress. A scripture my Pastor quotes is Matthew 11:12: " The kingdom of heaven suffers violence, and the violent take it by force." It's time for us to take back everything the accuser stole! Your relationship with THE FATHER, your prayer life, your sacrificial yes, your boldness, your manhood, your promise, your vision, your purpose, your fire and your position in the kingdom! Like my mother would say " I double dog dare you", to take it back! The Messiah is coming back for a church without a spot or a wrinkle and we as the head in whom dominion was given have to be in position and prepared for His return.


Adam, Where Are Thou?

Made in the USA
Middletown, DE
28 June 2022

67689743R00036